EXECUTIVE SUMMARY

Yemen is a republic with a constitution that provides for a president, a parliament, and an independent judiciary. Former president Ali Abdullah Saleh stepped down in 2012 when voters elected Abd Rabbuh Mansour Hadi, the sole consensus candidate, as president in a vote generally considered free and fair. The transitional government sought to expand political participation to excluded groups, including women, youth, and minorities. Progress ended in 2014, when Houthi rebels allied with forces loyal to former president Saleh (Houthi-Saleh rebels), staged an armed takeover against the government, precipitating its exile. The Houthis, in cooperation with Saleh's political party, the General People's Congress (GPC), then proceeded to take over many government functions and institutions in Sana'a. In August they announced the formation of a "Supreme Political Council," followed by the formation of a "National Salvation Government" in November. Neither body was recognized by the international community.

Civilian authorities did not maintain effective control over security forces. The government exercised limited control over military and security forces due to Houthi-Saleh rebel control over most of the security apparatus and state institutions. Competing family, tribal, party, and sectarian influences also reduced government authority.

The conflict between Houthi-Saleh rebels and forces loyal to the internationally recognized Hadi-led government continued throughout the year. Saudi Arabia and a coalition of other states continued air and ground operations against the Houthi-Saleh rebels. A UN-led peace process involving the government, the Houthis, and Saleh's GPC did not produce a peace agreement or a sustained cessation of hostilities. As of November the Hadi-led government had re-established a steady presence in Aden as well as an intermittent presence in some other governorates but had not returned to the capital Sana'a and remained unable to re-establish fully the rule of law in the territory it holds.

The most significant human rights problems were violence committed by various groups, weak and failing state institutions that allowed widespread disregard for the rule of law, and the inability of citizens to choose their government through free and fair elections.

Other human rights abuses included killings, disappearances, kidnappings, and reports of the use of excessive force and torture by security forces and various militant groups; cruel, inhuman, or degrading treatment or punishment; poor prison conditions; arbitrary arrest and detention; lengthy pretrial detentions; infringements on citizens' privacy rights; limits on freedom of expression, press, assembly, association, and movement; limits on freedom of religion, particularly for members of the Bahai community; lack of government transparency; corruption; violence and discrimination against women, children, persons with disabilities, and minorities; use of child soldiers; restrictions on worker rights; and trafficking in persons, including forced labor.

Impunity was persistent and pervasive. Houthi-Saleh influence over government institutions severely reduced the government's capacity to conduct investigations.

Nonstate actors committed significant abuses while engaged in internal armed conflict, including: Houthi-Saleh rebels; tribal militias; resistance forces; militant secessionist elements; al-Qaeda in the Arabian Peninsula (AQAP); and a local branch of Da'esh. Few actions led to prosecutions. Saudi-led coalition airstrikes resulted at times in high numbers of civilian casualties and damage to infrastructure, including hospitals. The Saudi-led coalition's Joint Incident Assessment Team (JIAT) investigated some incidents, although its reports did not lead to prosecutions. Government and Saudi-led coalition delays or denials of permits for commercial and aid shipments bound for rebel-held ports, as well as Houthi rebels' disruptions of aid delivery, exacerbated the humanitarian situation; a reported 69 percent of the population required some form of humanitarian assistance as of November.

Section 1. Respect for the Integrity of the Person, Including Freedom from:

a. Arbitrary Deprivation of Life and other Unlawful or Politically Motivated Killings

There were numerous unconfirmed reports that current or former members of the security forces committed arbitrary or unlawful killings. Politically motivated killings by nonstate actors, including Houthi-Saleh rebel forces and terrorist and insurgent groups claiming affiliation with AQAP or Da'esh, increased significantly during the year (see section 1.g.).

According to Human Rights Watch (HRW), in midyear men in civilian clothes took a doctoral student in Sana'a to a nearby Houthi-controlled police station. In

August relatives of the student were told he had been killed. After seeing the body in the morgue, a family member claimed that it showed signs of torture, including burn marks.

In an August report, the UN Office of the High Commissioner for Human Rights (OHCHR) claimed that AQAP, Da'esh, and affiliated militants often targeted members of security forces, judicial authorities, and civilians. The OHCHR documented 27 killings in Aden in January, most of which were perpetrated by unknown armed groups or militants affiliated with AQAP or Da'esh.

In January media outlets reported that AQAP publicly stoned a woman to death in Mukalla after accusing her of adultery and prostitution.

On March 4, unknown militants killed 16 civilians in a senior citizens' home run by Christian nuns in the Sheikh Othman area of Aden, according to media reports.

Da'esh claimed responsibility for a series of attacks on Houthi-affiliated Shia mosques. In June Da'esh killed at least 42 persons, mostly soldiers and one child, and injured five civilians with four suicide car bombings at security targets in Hadramawt Province, media reported.

b. Disappearance

During the year there were reports of politically motivated disappearances and kidnappings of individuals associated with political parties, nongovernmental organizations (NGOs), and media outlets critical of various security forces within the government and critical of the Houthi movement (see section 1.g.). Houthi-Saleh rebels and their allies sometimes detained civilian family members of government security officials. Nonstate actors targeted foreigners, including those believed to be working for foreign diplomatic missions.

Abductions were difficult for foreign entities to verify unless they involved a foreigner or government official. Many unofficial groups abducted persons to achieve specific goals. The local Mwatana Organization for Human Rights reported in May that Houthi authorities carried out 26 cases of enforced disappearance.

In December 2015 unidentified gunmen kidnapped a Tunisian woman, Nourane Hawas, in Sana'a while she was working for the International Committee of the Red Cross (ICRC). Hawas was released on October 3.

On September 20, Houthi rebels abducted an American teacher from an English-language school in Sana'a, media reported. He was released on October 15.

On October 21, media outlets reported that an Australian soccer coach working in Sana'a appeared in a video claiming to have been kidnapped by an unnamed group.

c. Torture and Other Cruel, Inhuman, or Degrading Treatment or Punishment

The constitution prohibits torture and other such abuses. Although the law lacks a comprehensive definition of torture, there are provisions allowing prison terms of up to 10 years for acts of torture. There were reports of torture committed by various groups during the year.

Torture and other forms of mistreatment were common in Houthi-Saleh detention facilities and by Houthi-Saleh rebels in informal facilities, according to the government's National Commission to Investigate Alleged Violations to Human Rights (NCIAVHR), based in Aden. The government established the NCIAVHR in September 2015, and its membership includes judges and legal and other human rights experts. The commission stated in its August report that it had received reports of 132 cases of torture during the year. In November HRW documented 11 cases of alleged torture and other mistreatment, including the abuse of a child, by Houthi-Saleh rebels in Sana'a.

The OHCHR reported that, during their visit to the Houthi rebel-affiliated Popular Committee-controlled Women's Central Prison in Sana'a in February, four women detainees claimed they had been blindfolded during their capture and taken to an unidentified location, where they were subjected to electric shocks and accused of being prostitutes.

During the year Houthi-Saleh rebels arrested and detained a 17-year-old high school student, who claimed to have been beaten and threatened while being interrogated for hours about his family's links to opposition parties. According to HRW, he was released after a month.

HRW reported that in August 2015 Houthi-Saleh rebels arrested and detained Abd al-Kader al-Guneid, a medical doctor and human rights activist. While detained, al-Guneid examined and treated other detainees with injuries he suspected were the result of mistreatment or torture, including a man with paralyzed arms and legs, cigarette burns, and a castrated testicle. Al-Guneid was released in May.

Prison and Detention Center Conditions

Prison conditions were harsh and life threatening and did not meet international standards. Prisoners lacked many basic needs. The Hadi-led government exercised very limited control over prison facilities. In past years government officials and NGOs identified overcrowding, lack of professional training for corrections officials, poor sanitation, inadequate access to justice, intermingling of pretrial and convicted inmates, lack of effective case management, lack of funding, and deteriorating infrastructure as problems within the 18 central prisons and 25 reserve prisons (also known as pretrial detention centers). According to the OHCHR, in August former detainees reported that they faced squalid sanitation conditions and were deprived of adequate food and medical care and not allowed outside visitors. Authorities held prisoners with physical or mental disabilities with the general population without special accommodations.

Beginning in late 2014, Houthi-Saleh rebels seized control of most prisons and released many convicted criminals; they also engineered several jailbreaks from facilities they did not control. Under Houthi-Saleh rebel management, prisons and other places of detention failed to meet minimum health or hygiene standards, according to monitors from the state-affiliated Yemeni Coalition to Monitor Human Rights Violations who visited Houthi-run facilities in Sana'a in 2015. According to the OHCHR, the Houthi-Saleh rebel-affiliated popular committees operated at least eight detention facilities in Sana'a, including Habra in al-Shu'aub District, Hataresh in Bani Hashaysh District, al-Thawra and the House of Ali Mohsen al-Ahmar in Haddah.

Tribes in rural areas operated unauthorized "private" prisons and detention centers based on traditional tribal justice. Tribal leaders sometimes placed "problem" tribesmen in private jails, sometimes simply rooms in a sheikh's house, to punish them for noncriminal actions. Tribal authorities often detained persons for personal or tribal reasons without trial or judicial sentencing.

Physical Conditions: The continuing conflict negatively affected the condition of prisons. Observers described most prisons, particularly in rural areas, as overcrowded, with poor sanitary conditions, inadequate food and access to potable water, and inadequate medical care. Limited information was available on prison populations during the year.

Prior to the outbreak of the conflict, local NGOs reported that prison authorities held juveniles with adults in some rural and women's prisons as well as in some prisons in the capital. By custom young children and infants born in prison remained in custody with their mothers until age nine. Prison authorities performed pregnancy tests on all female prisoners upon entry into a facility. Prisons segregated male and female adult prisoners and subjected them to similar conditions.

Political prisoners reportedly faced torture, abuse, and other forms of mistreatment, while all prisoners experienced harsh physical conditions. Houthi-Saleh rebels reportedly hung detainees upside down, beat them repeatedly, and pulled their hair, according to former detainees.

No credible statistics were available on the number of inmate deaths during the year. The NCIAVHR documented two incidents in which victims died as a result of torture by Houthi rebels after being released from short-term detention, one in December 2015 and one in April. HRW published a report in November that noted the deaths of two detainees held by Houthi rebels.

Administration: Limited information was available on prison administration after the Houthi-Saleh rebel takeover in 2014. Poor recordkeeping and a lack of communication between prisons and the central government made it difficult for authorities to estimate accurately the size of the prison population. Prior to the government's exile, a restructuring of prison administration also impeded improvement in recordkeeping.

In 2014 the NGO National Organization for Defending Rights and Freedoms (also called HOOD) claimed that bribery and corruption played major roles in prison mismanagement and that prisoners who paid bribes received better services and benefits. Many prisoners faced prolonged stays in detention beyond their sentences if they or their families could not pay fines or provide expected bribes.

There was no ombudsman to serve on behalf of prisoners and detainees. Under past practice, prisoners could submit complaints to judicial authorities; according to NGO reports, authorities largely ignored such complaints. Authorities generally allowed prisoners and detainees visitors when family members knew a detainee's location but granted limited access to family members of security-offense prisoners and detainees. They generally allowed prisoners and detainees to engage in religious observances.

According to a November HRW report, the general prosecutor of the Houthi-Saleh-controlled Ministry of Justice had ordered investigations into alleged abuse and the release of dozens of detainees held by Houthi and Saleh forces, but in most cases prison and police authorities ignored the orders and often blocked access to prisons by officials meant to oversee detainees. Saleh al-Sammad, president of the rebel-backed Supreme Political Council, issued a decree on September 21 providing amnesty to those who had helped the Saudi-led coalition. There was little information, however, on whether the Houthi-Saleh rebels effectively implemented this decree.

Independent Monitoring: The continuing conflict prevented substantial prison monitoring by independent human rights observers.

The OHCHR visited detention facilities controlled by the Houthis and Houthi-affiliated popular committees in seven governorates in November and December 2015 and visited the Houthi-controlled Women's Central Prison in Sana'a in February. The ICRC was unable to visit detention facilities during the year. Other international organizations and human rights groups also reported that they were denied access to Houthi-held detention facilities.

d. Arbitrary Arrest or Detention

The law prohibits arbitrary arrest and detention, but both continued to occur. The law prohibits arrests or serving subpoenas between sundown and dawn, but local NGOs reported that authorities took some persons suspected of crimes from their homes at night without warrants. Security forces remained largely under the control of Houthi rebels as of year's end.

In June media reported Houthi and pro-Saleh forces were holding 3,760 detainees. In May Amnesty International (AI) published a report examining 60 cases of detention and disappearance by Houthi rebels since September 2014. Seventeen of those detained remain in custody without being charged or tried. Since August 2014, HRW has documented 61 cases of arbitrary or abusive detention by Houthi and Saleh forces. HRW reported in November that at least 26 had since been released, 24 remained in custody, two died during detention, and nine appeared to have been forcibly disappeared with their whereabouts unknown.

The local Mwatana Organization for Human Rights issued a report in May claiming it had documented 53 cases of arbitrary detention by Houthi-Saleh rebels since September 2014. According to Mwatana, these detentions ranged from days to several months in length, and many of the detainees were journalists, activists, academics, and political figures who had voiced criticism of the Houthi-Saleh rebel takeover. Members and affiliates of the al-Islah political party were also detained.

Role of the Police and Security Apparatus

The primary state security and intelligence-gathering entities, the Political Security Organization (PSO) and the National Security Bureau (NSB), came under Houthi-Saleh rebel control in late 2014, although their structure and operations appeared to remain the same. The Hadi-led government, however, maintained its own appointments to the PSO and NSB in the areas under government control, similar to other dual or parallel structures of institutions in the country. By law the PSO and NSB report first to the minister of interior and then to the president. The relationship and coordination efforts between the NSB and PSO were unclear. There was no clear definition of many of the NSB's priorities. The law charges the PSO with identifying and combating political crimes and acts of sabotage.

The Criminal Investigation Division reports to the Ministry of Interior and conducted most criminal investigations and arrests. The ministry's paramilitary Special Security Force (SSF), often responsible for crowd control, was under the direct authority of the interior minister, as was the counterterrorism unit. The Ministry of Defense also employed units under its formal supervision to quell domestic unrest and to participate in internal armed conflicts.

Impunity for security officials remained a problem, in part because the Hadi-led government exercised limited authority and in part due to the lack of effective mechanisms to investigate and prosecute abuse and corruption. The SSF, the Yemen Special Operations Forces, the Presidential Guard (formerly the Republican Guard), the NSB, and other security organs ostensibly reported to civilian authorities in the Ministry of Interior, Ministry of Defense, and the Office of the President. Civilian control of these agencies continued to deteriorate, however, as rebel actors undid restructuring efforts inspired by the Gulf Cooperation Council Initiative (GCC-I), a regional effort to promote national reconciliation. Exacerbating the problem of impunity, interest groups, including former president Saleh's family and other tribal and party entities, expanded their influence over these agencies, often through unofficial channels rather than through the formal command structure.

Arrest Procedures and Treatment of Detainees

Upon its exile in 2015 and continuing during the year, the Hadi-led government lost control over much of the court or prison systems, and both systems deteriorated. The law provides that authorities cannot arrest an individual unless they apprehend him while he was committing a criminal act or have served him with a summons. In addition, authorities must arraign a detainee within 24 hours or release him. The judge or prosecuting attorney, who decides whether detention is required, must inform the accused of the basis for the arrest. The law stipulates authorities may not hold a detainee longer than seven days without a court order. There was no confirmed information on whether the law was respected during the year.

The law contains provisions for bail, but no information was available on its application; in the past some authorities allowed bail only if they received a bribe. The law prohibits incommunicado detention, provides detainees the right to inform their families of their arrest, and allows detainees to decline to answer questions without an attorney present, but no information was available on whether authorities respected these provisions; in the past authorities did not always respect these rights. The law states the government must provide attorneys for indigent detainees, but no information was available on whether this occurred; in the past the government often did not do so. Tribal mediators commonly settled rural cases without reference to the formal court system.

Detainees often did not know which investigating agency arrested them, and the agencies frequently complicated matters by unofficially transferring custody of individuals between entities. Prior to the rebel takeover, security forces routinely detained relatives of fugitives as hostages until the fugitive was located. Authorities stated that they detained relatives only when the relatives obstructed justice, but human rights organizations rejected this claim.

Arbitrary Arrest: Prior to the outbreak of conflict, the government routinely practiced arbitrary arrest, and the Houthi-Saleh rebels who seized power did the same. The number of persons arrested arbitrarily was difficult to estimate. Even prior to the outbreak of conflict, authorities did not record many detainees' names, did not transfer some detainees to official detention centers, and arrested and released many detainees multiple times during the year. In many areas, Houthi-Saleh and their allies arbitrarily detained persons and kept them in temporary prisons, including at military sites. Other nonstate actors also arbitrarily detained persons.

NGOs reported that Houthi-Saleh rebel forces detained individuals without judicial orders and denied them family visits or legal representation. On August 10, AI reported that Houthi-Saleh-controlled NSB officers arrested and detained 65 individuals from a Bahai youth workshop in Sana'a. One of those arrested remained imprisoned at year's end.

Pretrial Detention: Very limited information was available on pretrial detention practices during the year. Prior to the outbreak of the conflict, international monitoring organizations estimated that half of the detainees held by the Ministry of Interior either awaited trial or were pending investigation. Prolonged detentions without charge or, if charged, without a public preliminary judicial hearing within a reasonable time were common practices, despite their prohibition by law. Staff shortages, judicial inefficiency, and corruption caused trial delays.

Detainee's Ability to Challenge Lawfulness of Detention before a Court: Information was limited on whether persons arrested or detained were entitled to challenge the legal basis of their detention in court. Although the law provides that authorities must arraign a detainee within 24 hours or release him and that the judge or prosecuting attorney must inform the accused of the basis for the arrest, the government lacked the capacity to enforce the law after the start of the conflict.

In its May report, Mwatana claimed that those detained by the Houthi-Saleh rebels were often not briefed on the charges against them. In some cases, detainees who were issued release orders from the Houthi-controlled courts had yet to be released.

e. Denial of Fair Public Trial

Upon its exile in 2015 and during the year, the Hadi-led government lost control over much of the court system to Houthi-Saleh rebels, who continued to operate these institutions during the year. The constitution provides for an independent judiciary, but the judiciary was weak, not fully independent, and hampered by corruption, political interference, and lack of proper legal training. Judges' social and political affiliations and occasional bribery influenced verdicts. Prior to the outbreak of the conflict, the government's lack of capacity and reluctance at times to enforce court orders, especially outside the cities, further undermined the credibility of the judiciary. Criminals threatened and harassed members of the judiciary to influence cases.

Trial Procedures

The law considers defendants innocent until proven guilty. Trials were generally public, but all courts may conduct closed sessions "for reasons of public security or morals." Judges, who play an active role in questioning witnesses and the accused, adjudicate criminal cases. Defendants have the right to be present and to consult with an attorney in a timely manner. Defendants can confront or question witnesses against them and present witnesses and evidence on their behalf. The law provides for the government to furnish attorneys for indigent defendants in serious criminal cases, but no information was available on whether this occurred; in the past, the government did not always provide counsel in such cases. Defendants and their attorneys in principle had access to government-held evidence relevant to their cases, and authorities allowed defense attorneys to counsel their clients, address the court, and examine witnesses and any relevant evidence. Defendants have the right to appeal, and the slow pace of court cases provided adequate time to prepare a defense. Defendants could not be compelled to testify or confess guilt. During the year there was limited information available regarding respect for due process.

A court of limited jurisdiction considers security cases. A specialized criminal court, the State Security Court, operated under different procedures in closed sessions and did not provide defendants the same rights provided in the regular courts. Defense lawyers reportedly did not have full access to their clients' charges, relevant government-held evidence, or court files. The lack of birth registration compounded difficulties in proving age, which reportedly led courts to sentence juveniles as adults, including for crimes eligible for death sentences (see section 6, Children).

In addition to established courts, there is a tribal justice system for noncriminal issues. Tribal judges, usually respected neutral sheikhs, often also adjudicated criminal cases under tribal law, which usually involved public accusation without the formal filing of charges. Tribal mediation often emphasized social cohesion more than punishment. The results carried the same weight as court judgments, if not more, because the public often respected the tribal process more than a formal court system seen by many as corrupt and lacking independence.

Court proceedings continued in the case of Hamed Kamal bin Haydara, a Bahai, detained in 2013 by the NSB. Security officials reportedly accused him of apostasy, proselytizing, and spying for Israel. Bin Haydara reported authorities tortured him during the first 45 days of his detention. Following the outbreak of the conflict, Houthi-Saleh rebels kept bin Haydara imprisoned and continued court proceedings against him. NGOs claimed the prosecutor in the case made derogatory statements against the Bahai faith in the courtroom on several occasions. Bin Haydara faced charges for committing "an act that violates the independence of the republic," insulting Islam, and apostasy, which could be punishable by death. At Bin Haydara's November hearing, the judge reportedly asked him questions on his citizenship, the functioning of, and his relationship to, the elected governing bodies of the Bahai community of Yemen, and whether there were any witnesses to his claims of being tortured and forced to sign blindly documents, using his fingerprints, while in prison. Bin Haydara remained in detention at year's end.

Political Prisoners and Detainees

There were numerous reports of political prisoners and detainees, although confirmation of the number and status of political prisoners or detainees was difficult. Following their takeover of state institutions, rebels detained activists, journalists, demonstration leaders, and other political figures representing various political groups and organizations opposed to the Houthi-Saleh rebels. They did not charge detainees publicly, and they severely restricted or barred information to and access by local or international human rights organizations. Absent public charges, it was often difficult to determine whether authorities held detainees for criminal or political activity.

In May, 10 journalists detained by Houthi-Saleh rebels since 2015 began a hunger strike to protest their mistreatment, which included beatings and denial of access to medical treatment, visits, and adequate nutrition, according to an October report by the Gulf Center for Human Rights (GCHR). HRW reported that the journalists were moved to PSO headquarters in May, where they remained in detention.

Civil Judicial Procedures and Remedies

The law provides a limited ability to pursue civil remedies for human rights violations as tort claims against private persons. There were no reports of such efforts during the year. Citizens cannot sue the government directly but may petition the public prosecutor to initiate an investigation.

f. Arbitrary or Unlawful Interference with Privacy, Family, Home, or Correspondence

The law prohibits these actions, but authorities continued such interference. According to human rights NGOs, rebel security actors searched homes and private offices, monitored telephone calls, read personal mail and e-mail, and otherwise intruded into personal matters without legally issued warrants or judicial supervision.

Both before and after the armed takeover, the attorney general was required personally to authorize telephone call monitoring and reading of personal mail and e-mail; information was not available on whether this practice continued following the start of the conflict. Once exiled, the government lost control over security institutions for the most part and exercised limited to no control in rebel-held areas. The government continued to struggle with capacity and governance issues, even in the limited areas it controlled.

Citizens may not marry a foreigner without permission from the Ministry of Interior, the NSB, and, in some instances, the PSO, under a regulation authorities enforced arbitrarily. In the past the government enacted regulations to reduce a form of sex tourism in which significant numbers of foreigners, particularly Saudis and Emiratis, entered into temporary marriages with young Yemeni women (as is possible under Islamic law). They then left the bride, frequently pregnant and without means of support, to return to their countries of origin, where they would terminate the temporary marriage (see section 6, Women). The ministry typically approved marriages to foreigners if the foreigner provided an embassy letter stating that the government of the non-Yemeni spouse had no objection to the marriage and presented a marriage contract signed by a judge. Bribes frequently facilitated approval. There was no available information on current practice.

g. Abuses in Internal Conflict

In late 2014 Houthi-Saleh rebels took control of the capital and much of the functions and institutions of government, precipitating the exile of President Hadi and his government in March 2015. The ensuing conflict continued as of year's end. The UN-led peace process included several attempts to maintain a cessation of hostilities at various intervals throughout the year, but little progress was made. Throughout the year the Saudi-led coalition also continued military operations against Houthi-Saleh rebels, although a cessation of hostilities coinciding with UN-led peace talks in Kuwait largely held between April and August. The cessation of hostilities broke down after the suspension of the talks in August, and all sides resumed military operations. During the year the United Arab Emirates (UAE) continued an active military role in Yemen as a part of the Saudi-led coalition, including conducting ground operations against AQAP in Mukalla.

The Hadi-led government re-established a presence in Aden as well as some other areas late in the year. Prime Minister Ahmed Bin Dagher and part of the cabinet remained in Aden as of October, with some of the cabinet also in Marib; President Hadi remained primarily in Aden since late in the year.

Throughout the year clashes occurred as the parties expanded control over, lost, and regained territory. The military's loyalty was divided among numerous local actors. Armed clashes continued and expanded to several areas of the country among Houthi-Saleh rebels, supporters of both the Islah Party (Sunni Islamist) and the Rashad Party (Salafi), armed separatists affiliated with the southern separatist movement Hirak tribal forces, progovernment resistance forces, and some Saudi-led coalition ground forces, with participation by elements of the Hadi-led government's armed forces. Terrorist groups, including AQAP and Da'esh, carried out many deadly attacks against government representatives and installations, Houthi combatants, members of Hirak, and other actors accused of behavior violating sharia law.

Yemeni and international observers criticized all parties to the conflict for civilian casualties and damage to infrastructure resulting from shelling and airstrikes.

As a result of the fighting, the humanitarian situation in the country deteriorated significantly, with 14.1 million food insecure persons and a reported 69 percent of the country's population requiring humanitarian assistance by the end of the year, according to the United Nations. In January the United Nations reported that 500,000 children face life-threatening malnutrition. According to the World Bank, "chronic drug shortages, unpaid salaries, and conflict-related destruction restricted around 14 million Yemenis, including 8.3 million children, from accessing health-care services."

Killings: Civilians died from Saudi-led coalition airstrikes and reportedly indiscriminate shelling of civilian areas. While information on civilian casualties was incomplete, especially with the closure of many health facilities during the year due to insecurity and the lack of supplies, NGOs, media outlets, and humanitarian and international organizations reported on what they characterized as disproportionate and indiscriminate use of force by all parties to the continuing conflict.

The OHCHR estimated that, between March 2015 and August 23, some 3,799 civilians were killed and 6,711 injured as a result of the conflict, with more than three million displaced. The OHCHR further estimated that approximately one-third of these deaths were attributable to Saudi-led coalition airstrikes, with civilian casualties also resulting from shelling by Houthi-Saleh rebels and their affiliated popular committees. Other deaths resulted from attacks and killings by armed groups, including Al Qaeda and Da'esh.

According to the government's NCIAVHR, Houthi rebels fired two projectiles in June 2015 that struck a college dorm building and a residential area in Al Sha'b, killing six civilians and injuring 38 others.

Between June 3 and 8, rocket and mortar attacks originating from an area of Ta'iz controlled by the popular committees and forces loyal to Saleh killed 18 civilians and injured 68 others, according to OHCHR reports.

Houthi militias and forces allied with Saleh fired long-range missiles into or towards Saudi Arabia nearly 30 times between January 1 and September 21, according to the Center for Strategic and International Studies and media reports. Saudi media reported that more than 370 Saudi civilians were killed along the Saudi-Yemen border since March 2015.

The Saudi-led coalition airstrikes resulted in civilian casualties and damage to infrastructure on multiple occasions. The United Nations and NGOs, including HRW and AI, voiced concerns regarding Saudi-led coalition activities, claiming some coalition airstrikes were disproportionate or indiscriminate and appeared not to sufficiently minimize collateral impact on civilians. Coalition sources sometimes reported that damage in a given explosive incident resulted not from airstrikes but from shelling by Houthi-Saleh rebel forces; there were often contrary claims by pro-Houthi media. Due to continuing fighting, there was limited opportunity for post-incident forensic investigations.

On January 24, a Saudi-led coalition airstrike destroyed nine houses and killed a judge and seven members of his family in the Nahdah neighborhood outside Sana'a, according to OHCHR reports.

During the year that ended on June 30, the OHCHR documented five attacks on markets by the Saudi-led coalition. On March 15, Saudi-led coalition airstrikes reportedly killed 107 civilians, injured 37, and destroyed 16 shops in a market in Mustaba District of Hajjah Governorate.

On August 20, the OHCHR reported that a Saudi-led coalition airstrike in a residential area near the residence of Saleh in Ta'iz killed 53 civilians, including 28 children, and injured 11 others.

On October 8, media and human rights organizations reported that a Saudi-led coalition airstrike hit a crowded funeral hall in Sana'a, killing at least 140 persons and wounding more than 500 others, including children.

The NCIAVHR investigated and documented some incidents of airstrikes and shelling in its August report, which contained general recommendations on civilian protection, the nonuse of residential areas as bases and launch points for military operations, and the nonuse of land mines. The NCIAVHR's report did not lead to any prosecutions.

The Saudi-led coalition's JIAT, based in Riyadh and consisting of 14 military and civilian members from coalition member states, investigated some incidents of airstrikes that reportedly resulted in civilian casualties and claims by international organizations that humanitarian aid convoys and infrastructure were targeted by the coalition. On December 7, JIAT released summaries of reports of five incidents, including the August 15 attack against a Doctors without Borders (MSF) facility in the Abs District of Hajjah Governorate. In August JIAT released a press statement with summary findings of eight investigations. JIAT also issued a press statement on its initial investigation of the October 8 funeral-hall airstrike, claiming that a Yemeni source passed the coalition information that inaccurately reported the funeral hall was a military target. JIAT recommended that action be taken against those who caused the incident. It also recommended that the coalition review its rules of engagement and that families of the victims receive compensation. In addition, JIAT recommended in two separate incidents an investigation into potential violations of the rules of engagement and that individuals involved in two other incidents be held accountable. JIAT's investigations did not lead to any prosecutions as of year's end.

Abductions: In its August report, the OHCHR stated that it verified 491 cases of abduction and "deprivation of liberty" since July 2015. Of these, 89 percent were allegedly committed by the Popular Committees, 6 percent by AQAP affiliates, and 5 percent by the Popular Resistance Committees. The OHCHR reported that, as of March 24, some 249 individuals, including 18 journalists, were reportedly detained without cause in detention facilities throughout the country. Tribal groups were also responsible for kidnappings for ransom, as were other nonstate actors, such as AQAP (see section 1.b.).

On October 30, three Saudi-led coalition airstrikes damaged a Houthi-held detention facility and military base in Hudaydah, reportedly killing 63 persons, many of whom were detained by Houthi rebels, according to HRW.

Local press reports and activists have also alleged that coalition and local Yemeni forces have abducted, arbitrarily detained, and mistreated individuals, including those without apparent ties to terrorist organizations, as part of their counterterrorism efforts in the Mukalla area.

<u>Physical Abuse, Punishment, and Torture</u>: The NCIAVHR claimed to have received 132 reports of torture since 2015 (see section 1.c.).

Media and NGOs reported that Houthi-Saleh forces used land mines in civilian areas in the governorates of Abyan, Aden, Marib, Lahij, and Ta'iz. On August 9, an antivehicle mine killed 11 civilians in Ta'iz, according to HRW. HRW reported that land mines killed at least 18 and wounded more than 39 persons in Ta'iz between May 2015 and April 2016. In May AI reported several incidents in which children were injured or killed playing with unexploded ordinance that they mistook for toys.

In August the Yemen Executive Mine Action Center told HRW that its staff had cleared 32 antipersonnel mines and 25 antivehicle mines in Ta'iz since March. The Ta'iz National Association for Demining began work in early March and cleared land mines from at least 16 locations and destroyed 24 improvised explosive devices between March and April. The Hadi-led government and the Saudi-led coalition brought in an antimine team from Saudi Arabia and the UAE to clear land mines.

<u>Child Soldiers</u>: Although law and government policy expressly forbid the practice, children under the age of 18 directly participated in armed conflict for government, tribal, and militant forces, primarily as guards and couriers. Nearly one-third of the combatants in the country were younger than 18, by some estimates. The lack of a consistent system for birth registration compounded difficulties in proving age, which at times contributed to the recruitment of minors into the military. During the year the Houthis and other armed groups, including tribal and Islamist militias and AQAP, increased their recruitment, training, and deployment of children as participants in the conflict. In April the United Nations reported 762 verified cases of recruitment of boy soldiers, with 72 percent of incidents attributed

to Houthi-Saleh rebel forces, 15 percent to the Popular Committees, and 9 percent to AQAP.

Tribes, including some armed and financed by the government to fight alongside the regular army, used underage recruits in combat zones, according to reports by international NGOs such as Save the Children. Houthi-Saleh rebels routinely used children to operate checkpoints and search vehicles. Combatants reportedly involved married boys between the ages 12 and 15 in armed conflicts in the northern tribal areas. Tribal custom considers married boys as adults who owe allegiance to the tribe. As a result, according to international and local human rights NGOs, half of tribal fighters were youths under 18. Other observers noted that tribes rarely placed boys in harm's way but used them as guards rather than fighters.

The UN Security Council Panel of Experts on Yemen reported in January that young men and child combatants of all local fighting groups in Aden were reportedly subject to rape upon capture.

Also see the Department of State's annual *Trafficking in Persons Report* at www.state.gov/j/tip/rls/tiprpt/.

Other Conflict-related Abuses: There were reports of restrictions on the free passage of relief supplies and of humanitarian organizations' access to those individuals most in need perpetrated by all sides in the conflict. Supply interruptions made it difficult for aid agencies to support vulnerable populations. Increasing food insecurity, fuel shortages, damage to local infrastructure, and lack of access for humanitarian organizations to vulnerable populations contributed to the deteriorating humanitarian situation. Some media outlets reported that the government, the coalition, or both delayed or denied clearance permits for humanitarian and commercial aid shipments bound for rebel-held Red Sea ports.

Other sources reported that the Houthi-Saleh militias' forceful takeover and misadministration of government institutions led to dire economic consequences-- the nonpayment of workers' wages; unmaintained and unrepaired gantry cranes at ports where aid materiel was offloaded; and allegations of widespread corruption, including at checkpoints controlled by Houthi-Saleh militias--which severely impacted the distribution of food aid and exacerbated food insecurity. In April the United Nations reported 16 verified incidents of denial of humanitarian access, with 11 incidents attributed to Houthi forces.

Militias held trucks containing food, medical supplies, and aid equipment at checkpoints and prevented them from entering major cities. The humanitarian situation in the Ta'iz Governorate worsened as Houthi-affiliated forces prevented food, medical supplies, and fuel from entering the city. Without fuel to run generators, the State Water Foundation could not function, putting hundreds of thousands of civilians at risk of illness due to disruption to water and sanitation facilities.

According to an HRW report published in July, coalition airstrikes damaged many factories and structures used for humanitarian and economic purposes during the year. HRW reported that, on January 6, an airstrike damaged a hangar containing food products, including rice and sugar, at Hudaydah Port; on February 2 and 5, two airstrikes on a cement factory in Amran reportedly killed 15 civilians and damaged buildings around the factory; and, on August 11 and 12, airstrikes destroyed Aldarejh Bridge, used by the World Food Program to transport approximately 90 percent of its food deliveries for the northern governorates, forcing it to use alternate supply routes.

There were reports of attacks on health-care facilities. The UN Secretary-General's report, *Children and Armed Conflict Report*, released in April reported 59 verified incidents of attacks on 34 hospitals in 2015, with some facilities attacked multiple times, especially in Aden and Ta'iz. The majority of repeated attacks were attributed to Houthi rebels. According to the report, the Saudi-led coalition destroyed 15 health facilities in the governorate of Sa'ada. On August 15, a coalition airstrike destroyed a MSF hospital in Hajjah governorate, which MSF reported killed 19 persons, including one MSF staff member, and injured 24 individuals. Later that month, MSF announced it would evacuate its staff from six hospitals in northern Yemen because it could not receive assurances that its hospitals would not be bombed again.

There were reports of deliberate attacks on health-care workers. In January the UN Security Council Panel of Experts reported at least 29 documented attacks on hospitals by all sides of the conflict, one attack on an ambulance, and nine cases in which humanitarian organizations and aid agencies were targets between March 26 and December 20, 2015.

There were reports of use of civilians to shield combatants. Houthi-Saleh forces reportedly used captives as human shields at military encampments and ammunition depots under threat of Saudi-led coalition airstrikes, extracted forced pledges and confessions, and demanded ransoms from family members. In

January the UN Security Council Panel of Experts on Yemen identified reports of Houthi-Saleh forces using migrants and refugees as human shields in unused buildings in Aden that were previously targeted by airstrikes or where weapons caches were claimed to be stored. HRW claimed that Houthi militants had stationed armed men in the compound of the Noor Center for the Care and Rehabilitation of the Blind in Sana'a, which was damaged by a Saudi-led coalition airstrike that injured three civilians on January 5.

Section 2. Respect for Civil Liberties, Including:

a. Freedom of Speech and Expression

Although the constitution provides for freedom of speech and the press "within the limits of the law," the Press and Publications Law calls for journalists to uphold national unity and prohibits criticism of the head of state. Rebel actors did not respect the rights as provided, and the government was unable to enforce them.

Freedom of Speech and Expression: There were reports that Houthi-Saleh rebels suppressed speech critical of them.

In February Houthi-Saleh rebels abducted the editor of *al-Sahwa News*, Abdullah al-Minefi, from his home in Dhamar and his whereabouts remained unknown, according to a report from the GCHR.

Press and Media Freedoms: Prior to the outbreak of conflict, the transitional government approved legislation to regulate broadcasting and television channels, and radio stations proliferated. A number of domestic private stations operated under media production company permits, and several stations broadcast from abroad for domestic audiences.

Violence and Harassment: Rebel actors, including Houthi militias and forces loyal to former president Saleh, were primarily responsible for a campaign of violence and harassment against journalists, according to a report from the Yemen Journalists Syndicate, an affiliate of the International Federation of Journalists. The government was unable to take any substantive steps to protect journalists from violence and harassment (Nongovernmental Impact).

In multiple instances Houthi-Saleh rebels went to the homes of activists, journalists, and political leaders opposed to the Houthis and used arrest and other means to intimidate perceived opponents and to silence dissent. According to

HRW, authorities frequently compelled detainees to sign contracts promising not to affiliate themselves with groups their captors saw as opposed to the Ansar Allah movement.

Censorship or Content Restrictions: The government did not and could not counter the practice of censorship by rebel actors inside Yemen. During the year Houthi-controlled Ministry of Telecommunications and internet service providers reportedly systematically blocked websites and domains that authorities deemed critical of the Houthi agenda. The OHCHR reported that Houthi-Saleh rebels blocked 10 news websites, censored four satellite television channels, and blocked five newspapers from going to print during the year.

Prior to the government's exile, Customs Authority and Ministry of Culture officials occasionally confiscated foreign publications regarded as either pornographic or religiously objectionable, according to the Freedom Foundation. The government required book authors to obtain certification from the Ministry of Culture for publication and to submit copies to the ministry. Publishers sometimes refused to deal with an author who had not obtained certification. The ministry approved most books, but long delays were frequent. Both the ministry and the PSO monitored and sometimes removed books from stores. No information was available on practices following the government's departure.

Libel/Slander Laws: The law criminalizes criticism of the "person of the head of state," although not necessarily "constructive" criticism; the publication of "false information" that may spread "dissent and division among the people"; materials that may lead to "the spread of ideas contrary to the principles of the Yemeni revolution"; and "false stories intended to damage Arab and friendly countries or their relations" with the country. Citing these restrictions, the Specialized Press and Publications Court intimidated journalists with excessive prosecutions for criminal defamation prior to the government's exile. No information was available on the court's subsequent operations.

Nongovernmental Impact: Houthi-Saleh rebels and AQAP significantly inhibited freedom of expression and members of the press through violence and harassment. As of December 2015 and during the year, the Houthi-Saleh rebels controlled several state ministries responsible for press and communications, including the Ministry of Telecommunications. In that capacity, they selected items for formerly government-run broadcast and print media and did not allow reports critical of themselves.

From January through June, according to the Yemen Journalists Syndicate, Houthi-Saleh rebels and progovernment popular resistance forces and tribal militias were responsible for a range of abuses of media outlets. Houthi-Saleh rebels abducted, detained, prosecuted, or disappeared 24 media workers. There were two cases of journalists' and newspaper property being confiscated, and 13 websites were blocked. Rebel actors were primarily responsible for these abuses, although some cases involved other security forces and the Saudi-led coalition, according to a Yemen Journalists Syndicate report. The Committee to Protect Journalists reported that six journalists were killed during the year, one by explosives laid by pro-Houthi fighters, one killed in fighting between progovernment groups and rebels, two killed by pro-Houthi-Saleh forces in battle, and two killed in Saudi-led coalition airstrikes. According to Reporters without Borders, 14 journalists were held captive through year's end, some by Houthi rebels and some by AQAP.

In January Houthi rebels reportedly abducted al-Jazeera television correspondent Hamdi al-Bokari, fellow reporter Abdelaziz al-Sabri, and their driver Mounir al-Soubaie. They were freed 10 days later, according to Reporters without Borders.

According to Reporters without Borders, on May 8, southern militants attacked and looted the premises of the al-Shumo Foundation and its affiliate newspaper in Aden, *Akhbar al-Youm*.

Internet Freedom

The government did not have the capacity to uphold internet freedom. Censorship affected internet freedom, and there were notable cases of Houthi-Saleh rebel intrusion into cyberspace. The Houthi-controlled Public Telecommunications Corporation systematically blocked user access to websites and internet domains it deemed dangerous to the rebel actors' political agenda.

According to the International Telecommunication Union, 25.1 percent of the population used the internet in 2015, while 5.5 percent had internet access at home.

The OHCHR reported that the Houthi-controlled Popular Committees blocked 10 news websites and censored four satellite television channels. In October media outlets reported that the mobile messaging application WhatsApp appeared to be blocked by Houthi-Saleh rebels, along with Facebook and Skype. The Houthi-controlled Ministry of Telecommunications claimed the sites were not blocked but rather were offline due to local disruptions to internet service and damage to telecommunications infrastructure due to the conflict, particularly in Sana'a, Sa'ada, and Amran.

Academic Freedom and Cultural Events

Prior to the conflict, political parties frequently attempted to influence university academic appointments and faculty and student elections. They actively recruited new students into party branches specifically created as youth divisions (for example, the General People's Congress Youth Division and the al-Islah Youth Division), through which the parties could mobilize youth on campuses.

The NSB maintained permanent offices on campuses, reflecting continued government concern about security and, in some cases, controversial speech. Party-affiliated officials at the Ministry of Higher Education and academic institutions reviewed prospective university professors and administrators for political acceptability before hiring them and commonly showed favoritism toward supporters of specific political parties. There were no reported instances of censored curriculums or sanctioned professors or students; however, after their takeover, Houthi and other actors' incursions onto campuses and detentions of academics appeared designed to intimidate them as perceived opponents.

b. Freedom of Peaceful Assembly and Association

Freedom of Assembly

The law provides for freedom of assembly. The government was unable to prevent infringements on freedom of assembly by Houthi-Saleh rebels and their affiliates, who responded at times with excessive force to demonstrations and protests in various parts of the country.

In October international media reported that gunmen loyal to Houthi militias suppressed demonstrations in Sana'a organized by mothers to protest the treatment of their sons who had been detained by Houthi forces.

Freedom of Association

While the law provides for freedom of association, the government lacked the capacity to protect this right, and there were reports that Houthi-Saleh rebels harassed and shut down NGOs. The law regulates associations and foundations and outlines the establishment and activities of NGOs. Authorities required annual registration. The law exempts registered NGOs from taxes and tariffs and requires the government to provide a reason for denying an NGO registration, such as deeming an NGO's activities "detrimental" to the state. It forbids NGO involvement in political or religious activities. It permits foreign funding of NGOs. The law requires government observation of NGO internal elections. There were no known attempts by NGOs to register during the year.

The OHCHR documented 10 cases in which Houthi-Saleh rebels raided the premises of human rights organizations; international NGOs operating in Sana'a also reported scrutiny, surveillance, and raids by Houthi-Saleh rebels. According to media reports, the rebels shut down three Bahai organizations in connection with the August arrest of individuals at a youth workshop (see section 1.d.).

c. Freedom of Religion

See the Department of State's *International Religious Freedom Report* at www.state.gov/religiousfreedomreport/.

d. Freedom of Movement, Internally Displaced Persons, Protection of Refugees, and Stateless Persons

The law provides for freedom of internal movement, foreign travel, emigration, and repatriation.

Prior to 2014 the transitional government cooperated with the Office of the UN High Commissioner for Refugees (UNHCR) and other humanitarian organizations in providing protection and assistance to internally displaced persons (IDPs), refugees, returning refugees, asylum seekers, stateless persons, and other persons of concern. The Houthi takeover and the ensuing conflict, however, made it difficult for humanitarian organizations to reach many areas of the country due to security concerns. The Hadi-led government did not and could not enforce the law, even in government-controlled areas, due to capacity and governance issues.

According to UNHCR, the country's laws and policies were consistent with international standards, but the authorities' capacity to protect and assist persons in need was limited. No authority was able to provide services in some parts of the country.

Abuse of Migrants, Refugees, and Stateless Persons: In past years multiple NGOs reported that criminal smuggling groups built a large number of "camps" near the

Yemen-Saudi border city of Haradh, where militants held migrants for extortion and ransom.

UNHCR and partners continued to face challenges accessing detention centers. UNHCR negotiated with relevant ministries to find alternative means to monitor refugees and asylum seekers in detention.

UNHCR reported in July that it received access to more than 40 Eritreans and Ethiopians detained in Hudaydah and al-Mahwit Governorates, most of whom wished to seek asylum. On July 3, UNHCR reported that all detained Somalis holding government-issued refugee identification documents (more than 50 individuals) were reportedly released from Hudaydah central prison. By late July, 36 Eritrean asylum-seekers and approximately 200 Somalis (who did not have identification cards) remained in Hudaydah central prison. On July 2, UNHCR secured the release of six Somalis from the Al Mansura detention center in Aden.

In-country Movement: Rebel forces, resistance forces, elements of the army and security forces, and tribesmen maintained checkpoints on major roads. In many regions, especially in areas outside effective central security control, armed tribesmen frequently restricted freedom of movement, operating their own checkpoints, sometimes with military or other security officials, and often subjected travelers to physical harassment, extortion, theft, or short-term kidnappings for ransom. Damage to roads, bridges, and other infrastructure from the conflict also hindered the delivery of humanitarian aid and commercial shipments (see section 1.g., Other Conflict-related Abuses).

Social discrimination severely restricted women's freedom of movement. Women in general did not enjoy full freedom of movement, although restrictions varied by location. Some observers reported increased restrictions on women in conservative locations, such as Sa'ada. Oxfam reported that men at checkpoints increasingly insisted on adherence to the "mahram" system, the cultural obligation of women to be accompanied by male relatives in public, in areas controlled by radical Islamic groups, such as AQAP. The report also noted that female respondents ranked the key factor limiting women's freedom of movement as the lack of cultural acceptance, followed by lack of security (see section 6, Women).

Authorities required travel permits for all non-Yemeni nationals leaving Sana'a.

The OHCHR reported that local authorities evicted at least 155 persons from Aden following a "carry your identification" campaign that witnesses claimed was used to displace northerners who were later captured and forcibly transported out of Aden.

<u>Foreign Travel</u>: In the past women needed to have the permission of a male guardian, such as a husband, before applying for a passport or leaving the country. A husband or male relative could bar a woman from leaving the country by placing a woman's name on a "no-fly list" maintained at airports. Prior to the conflict, authorities strictly enforced this requirement when women traveled with children, but there were no reports of this requirement being enforced by authorities during the year. There were attempts, however, by Houthi rebels to impose similar restrictions on women's international travel. Given the deterioration of infrastructure and lack of security due to the conflict, many women reportedly declined to travel alone (see section 6, Women).

Internally Displaced Persons

According to the Task Force on Population Movement, co-led by UNHCR and the International Organization for Migration (IOM), there were more than 2.1 million IDPs as of November. The government's IDP registration system has been on pause since the escalation of the conflict in March 2015.

IDPs originated from all governorates and have dispersed throughout the country. Ta'iz hosted 66 percent (620,934 individuals) of the identified IDP population, while the neighboring governorates of Ibb and Lahj hosted the next largest IDP populations with 12 percent (111,384 individuals) and 6 percent (52,866 individuals), respectively. Approximately 86 percent of the total conflict-displaced population originated from the governorates of Ta'iz, Hajjah, Amanat Al Asimah, Sa'ada, and Sana'a, according to the Task Force on Population Movement.

Humanitarian organizations' access to IDPs was generally poor due to the continuing conflict; however, the ICRC and MSF maintained a presence in multiple locations throughout the country. According to the United Nations, humanitarian organizations, local NGOs, and charities that still functioned in the capital supported IDPs in Sana'a with food, shelter, and nonfood items. IDPs from Sa'ada reported limited access to cash for purchasing basic household items. Most IDPs were farmers and had no other means to earn an income while in Sana'a.

Prevention of distribution of humanitarian goods, armed robberies, theft of vehicles, and the looting of offices impeded humanitarian organizations' access to and support of IDPs.

There was a marked increase in food insecurity throughout the country, and rates of acute malnutrition were high among IDPs and other vulnerable groups (see section 1.g., Other Conflict-related Abuses).

The IOM reported that IDPs largely sought refuge with relatives or friends or rented accommodations, where many faced frequent threats of eviction due to late payments of rent. Others were housed in unconventional shelters in public or private buildings, such as schools, health facilities, or religious buildings, primarily in Ta'iz and Lahj. By June 30, UNHCR had provided more than 41,550 IDP households (some 261,700 individuals) with nonfood items and more than 12,600 households (some 88,450 individuals) with full emergency shelter kits in 16 of the country's 22 governorates.

Since July 2015 the Saudi government-run King Salman (KS) Relief agency set up a temporary camp for displaced persons in al-Abr District, 60 miles south of al-Wadiah border crossing. This camp provided services for as many as 3,000 IDPs, including electricity, air conditioning, and drinking water. Late in the year, however, KS Relief decided to close the camp due to security problems that included fires and the theft of electricity generators. As of year's end, the camp remained open due to bureaucratic delays in officially closing it.

Protection of Refugees

Yemen maintained open borders during the conflict and received refugees from a variety of countries. Many refugees became increasingly vulnerable due to the worsening security and economic situation in the country. Somali, Ethiopian, Eritrean, and other refugees shared in the general poverty and insecurity of the country.

UNHCR estimated that from January until November, despite the conflict, more than 100,000 refugees, asylum seekers, and migrants arrived in the country by sea, the majority from Ethiopia as well as from Somalia and other countries. Many were attempting to reach or return to Saudi Arabia for work, deceived by smugglers who told them the conflict in Yemen was over, according to UNHCR. UNHCR figures indicated there were approximately 268,000 refugees in the country as of June 30; as of November this included at least 90,000 Ethiopians and 17,000 Somalis. Due to the fighting, many had been displaced from Aden to the camp at Kharaz and towns in southern Yemen. The Hadi-led government could not provide physical protection to refugees, and many were held in detention centers operated by Houthi-Saleh rebels in the North and the government in the South. UNHCR claimed there were reports of refugees facing physical and sexual abuse as well as torture and forced labor and that many refugees were susceptible to trafficking.

In November the United Nations estimated that 178,000 persons had fled the country since the outbreak of conflict, some seeking to cross the border into Saudi Arabia, others to cross the Red Sea for Djibouti, Somalia, or other nearby countries, despite the difficulty and danger of the crossing. Approximately one-third of the persons who fled the country were citizens; others included Somali refugees, Ethiopians, Djiboutians, Sudanese, and other foreign nationals who had worked in Yemen prior to the conflict.

Access to Asylum: The country is a signatory to the 1951 Refugee Convention and its 1967 protocol; however, no law addresses the granting of refugee status or asylum, and there was no system for providing protection to asylum seekers. In past years the government provided automatic refugee status to Somalis who entered the country. There was no information available on whether this practice continued during the conflict. The majority of new arrivals during the year came from Ethiopia, with others from Eritrea, Iraq, Syria, and other countries recognized under UNHCR's mandate.

Refoulement: In September media outlets reported that UAE-supported Security Belt Forces deported more than 200 migrants, mostly Ethiopians, from Aden. In October an estimated 1,000 Ethiopian migrants escaped a detention center where approximately 1,400 Ethiopians were being held prior to deportation. The IOM reported that Hadi-led government authorities expelled more than 240 migrants between December 16 and 19, dropping them in the water off the Djibouti shore. Since mid-October, Hadi-led government authorities expelled more than 1,200 migrants, mostly Ethiopian, to Djibouti.

Freedom of Movement: Freedom of movement remained difficult for all in the country, including refugees, given the damage to roads, bridges, and basic infrastructure caused by the conflict. In addition, most of the country's airports have incurred significant damage or been closed, making travel difficult. In areas controlled by Houthi-Saleh rebels, "illegal" or unofficial checkpoints caused unnecessary delays or blocked the movement of individuals or goods.

Access to Basic Services: In camps in Sana'a and in the Kharaz camp in Lahj and the Basateen camp in Aden, UNHCR's partners, the International Medical Corps and the Charitable Society for Social Welfare, provided medical consultations and essential medicines to more than 2,530 refugees as well as to 1,800 IDPs, mental health and psychological support to approximately 310 refugees and 40 IDPs, HIV treatments and tests to some 160 individuals, life-saving and specialized referral services to 150 refugees, and reproductive health services to 165 pregnant refugees and 90 IDPs, as well as vaccines to 240 refugees and 45 IDP children.

Community outreach counselling and awareness sessions were provided to 1,350 refugees and 710 IDPs on various problems, including HIV, hygiene promotion, nutrition, vaccinations, measles, and dengue fever. At Mayfa'a Reception Center (Shabwah Governorate), 3,130 new arrivals received medical consultation and 8,600 new arrivals were vaccinated.

Section 3. Freedom to Participate in the Political Process

The law provides citizens with the ability to choose their government peacefully through free and fair periodic elections based on universal and equal suffrage. The outbreak of conflict interrupted a government-initiated new voter registration program. There have been no elections since the outbreak of conflict in 2014.

Elections and Political Participation

Recent Elections: Observers generally considered the one-candidate election conducted in 2012 to be free and fair. Elections for the presidency remained pending under the Gulf Cooperation Council Initiative (GCC-I), a regional effort to promote national reconciliation which superseded elements of the constitution and permitted the extension of President Hadi's term through the end of the transition. In 2014 political parties acting within the National Dialogue Conference (NDC) endorsed that extension, and President Hadi remained the legitimate holder of the office. Thirteen parties signed a Peace and National Partnership Agreement in September 2014 that temporarily ended the violence associated with the Houthi-Saleh rebel entrance into Sana'a and called for implementation of the NDC, including holding elections and establishing a new constitution.

In February 2015 Houthi-Saleh rebels declared the constitution null and void, illegally disbanded parliament, and announced the formation of the appointive Supreme Revolutionary Committee as the highest governing body. In August the Houthi-aligned GPC announced the formation of a Supreme Political Council and the reconvening of parliament in Sana'a, followed by the announcement of what they termed a "national salvation government" in November. The institutions did not receive international recognition as government bodies, and elections for parliament were not held during the year. Scheduling of the next elections awaited an end to the conflict and a peace settlement between the parties. The UN-led negotiations continued at year's end.

<u>Political Parties and Political Participation</u>: The law requires political parties to be national organizations that do not restrict their membership to residents of a particular region or to members of a given tribe, religious sect, class, or profession. The power-sharing agreement outlined in the 2011 GCC-I broke down as rebels drove the internationally recognized government from the country.

HRW reported that many of the 61 individuals they documented in arbitrary or abusive detention by Houthi-Saleh rebels since August 2014 appeared to have been arrested because of ties to the al-Islah party. On February 22, Houthi rebels arrested and detained Samir al-Dubiani for his ties to al-Islah, according to HRW. Local NGOs and media also reported that individuals tied with al-Islah have been arbitrarily detained in Mukalla by UAE-affiliated Security Belt forces.

<u>Participation of Women and Minorities</u>: The Hadi-led government has two women ministers. Women participated in the UN-led negotiation process throughout the year, although not in high numbers. As of year's end, one woman served as a delegate on the government's 12-person negotiation team and one on the GPC team.

Prior to the outbreak of conflict, the provisions that were agreed at the 2014 NDC included a 30 percent quota for women in all branches of government. Thirty percent of delegates to the 2013-14 NDC were women, and women chaired many committees and working groups. The NDC had one delegate representing the minority group commonly known as "Muhamasheen" or "Akhdam." According to some preconflict estimates, the Muhamasheen (an ethnic group largely descended from East Africans) comprised up to 10 percent of the population. Although only one of the 565 delegates was from the Muhamasheen, this representation was a first for the community.

Section 4. Corruption and Lack of Transparency in Government

While the law provides for criminal penalties for official corruption, the government was unable to implement the law effectively. There were reports of official corruption during the year. A burdensome process creates a separate legal system for the political elite. According to the constitution, approval of one-fifth of the members of parliament is necessary to conduct a criminal investigation on a deputy minister or higher-ranking official. The law then requires a two-thirds majority in parliament and presidential permission to bring criminal investigation results to the general prosecutor for indictment. The government did not use the procedure before Houthi rebels illegally disbanded parliament in February 2015.

Corruption: A culture of corruption is pervasive throughout the country, and observers reported petty corruption in nearly every government office. Job candidates were often expected to purchase their positions. Observers believed tax inspectors undervalued assessments and pocketed the difference. Many government officials and civil service employees received salaries for jobs they did not perform or multiple salaries for the same job. Corruption also regularly affected government procurement. Corruption and the black marketing of goods increased overall in parts of Houthi-controlled areas, particularly in institutions it controlled from Sana'a.

Recent analyses by impartial international and local observers, including Transparency International, agreed that corruption was a serious problem in every branch and level of government, and especially in the security sector. International observers presumed government officials benefited from insider arrangements, embezzlement, and bribes. Political leaders and most government agencies took negligible action to combat corruption.

The Central Organization for Control and Audit (COCA) is the national auditing agency for public expenditures and the investigative body for corruption. COCA had not presented a report to parliament before Houthi rebels illegally disbanded parliament in February 2015. Prior to the outbreak of conflict, the president was responsible for appointing COCA's top officials. In cases involving high-level officials, COCA submitted reports directly to the president, who had the power to refuse the reports. Since COCA's inception in 1999, authorities have prosecuted only low-ranking officials for corruption. It has not conducted any known investigations since February 2015.

Some police stations reportedly maintained an internal affairs section to investigate security force abuses, and citizens have the right to file complaints with the Prosecutor's Office. The Ministry of Interior had a fax line for citizens to file claims of abuse for investigation. No information was available on the number of complaints the ministry received or investigated or whether the mechanism still existed.

To combat fraud and corruption in the government payroll system, the government in 2014 implemented a plan to collect biometric information on all government employees, including soldiers and security forces, and to create a central registry designed to eliminate tens of thousands of fraudulent and duplicate names from the payroll. By the end of 2014, the registry included nearly half a million civil servants. It had reportedly identified 5,000 workers who illegally received more than one paycheck. The government suspended implementation of the plan following the armed Houthi takeover in February 2015. The government also suspended implementation of a payment system for soldiers and security forces via bank or post office accounts. Prior to the outbreak of conflict, that system bypassed paymasters who had previously paid soldiers in cash.

The independent Supreme National Authority for Combating Corruption (SNACC) received complaints and developed programs to raise awareness of corruption prior to the outbreak of conflict. It included a council of government, civil society, and private sector representatives. A lack of capacity, particularly in terms of financial analysis, hampered the SNACC. According to the government, the SNACC continued to operate "at minimal levels" during the year; however, no information was available on the number of complaints received or referrals for prosecution.

Financial Disclosure: The law requires annual disclosure of financial assets by all ministers, deputy ministers, agency heads, members of parliament, and Shura Council members. Filers are to provide disclosures to the SNACC for verification. The information was not publicly available. The SNACC may also request disclosures from any other government employee. The law does not require disclosure of assets of children or spouses. It provides for penalties for false filing of information. There was no information on whether officials complied with the law.

Public Access to Information: The country's "right of access to information" law requires establishment of an independent agency to respond to requests for information and resolve grievances when authorities deny requests. The government had not established the agency prior to the outbreak of conflict. Houthi-Saleh rebels established extralegal "resolution committees" and "monitoring committees" within ministries as part of their continued efforts to establish parallel government institutions.

The law normally requires the Ministry of Finance to publish the government budget online, in print, and in CD format. The government attempted to implement the 2014 budget on a month-by-month basis, as provided for under

Article 88 of the constitution, but faced severe financial constraints. It was unclear how much of the 2014 budget the government was able to implement throughout the year. Information related to contract awards, including geographical area, company, and terms of the contract, was publicly available through the High Tender Board website and announcements in state media prior to the outbreak of the conflict. Government spending, particularly at the local level and with respect to military and security, and data relating to extractive industries, were murky and difficult to trace.

The law provides for journalists to have some access to government reports and information, but the government did little to provide for accessibility or transparency.

Section 5. Governmental Attitude Regarding International and Nongovernmental Investigation of Alleged Violations of Human Rights

Prior to the outbreak of conflict, domestic and international human rights groups generally operated without outright government restriction, but lower-level government officials, particularly those in security organizations, were occasionally uncooperative and unresponsive to human rights groups' views and requests for information. Local and international organizations attempting to investigate human rights cases reported obstacles in accessing victims, prisoners, and prisons. International, regional, and local media published their reports.

Nonstate actors, including the Houthi-Saleh rebels, subjected domestic human rights NGOs to significant harassment during the year (see also section 2.b., Freedom of Association).

Government Human Rights Bodies: In 2014 multistakeholder working groups within the NDC focused on a wide spectrum of problems pertaining to human rights, including freedom of press and expression, women's and minority rights, and religious diversity. In September 2015 Presidential Decree Number 13 established an independent National Commission to Investigate Alleged Violations to Human Rights (NCIAVHR), which is responsible for investigating all human rights violations since 2011. Its chairman is Qaher Mustafa Ali Ibrahim, and it consists of eight members with legal, judicial, or human rights backgrounds. The NCIAVHR issued its first report of human rights violations on August 15 and held a press conference at the country's Ministry of Foreign Affairs, temporarily located in Riyadh.

Section 6. Discrimination, Societal Abuses, and Trafficking in Persons

Women

Rape and Domestic Violence: The law criminalizes rape, but it does not criminalize spousal rape because the law states that a woman may not refuse sexual relations with her husband. The government did not enforce the law against rape effectively. The punishment for rape is imprisonment for up to 25 years.

There were no reliable rape statistics, principally because of social stigma, fear of familial and societal retaliation, and a legal system largely stacked against survivors, which limited their willingness to report the crime. The situation was compounded by the breakdown of rule of law following the start of the conflict. Most rape victims did not report the crime due to fear of shaming the family, incurring violent retaliation by the perpetrator or a family member, or facing prosecution. By law authorities can prosecute rape victims on charges of fornication if authorities do not charge a perpetrator. There were no known cases during the year. According to law, without the perpetrator's confession, the rape survivor must provide four male witnesses to the crime.

The law states that authorities should execute a man if convicted of killing a woman. The penal code, however, allows leniency for persons guilty of committing an "honor" killing or violently assaulting or killing a woman for perceived "immodest" or "defiant" behavior. The law also allows for a substantially reduced sentence when a husband kills his wife and a man he believes to be involved in an extramarital affair with her. The law does not address other types of gender-based violence, such as beatings, forced isolation, imprisonment, and early and forced marriage.

The law provides women with protection against domestic violence, except spousal rape, under the general rubric of protecting persons against violence, but authorities did not enforce this provision effectively. Victims rarely reported domestic abuse to police. Spousal abuse generally was undocumented, but women's groups asserted that physical, emotional, and sexual abuse within marriage was widespread.

The tribal arbitration process rather than criminal courts usually adjudicated cases of violence against women due to the widespread perception, shared by authorities, that violence against women was a private, family matter. Some local female tribal experts argued that tribal arbitration is fairer for women, and victims often preferred it to the courts for that reason. Due to social pressures, authorities expected an abused woman to take her complaint to a male relative rather than to authorities, to intercede on her behalf or provide sanctuary. For these social reasons, as well as the corruption and inefficiency of the justice system, criminal proceedings in cases of domestic abuse were rare.

As of 2014 the Ministry of Public Health and Population and the Ministry of Human Rights maintained hotlines for complainants, although they had little capacity to act on complaints. The Ministry of Human Rights referred callers to various civil society organizations or foundations for assistance. It also referred complainants to the nongovernmental National Women's Union for assistance. The National Women's Union, which had chapters across the country, had at least one shelter. The general director of the Family Protection Unit reported that the unit rarely received complaints of violence against women. No information was available on the availability of hotlines or shelters during the year.

The continuing conflict and humanitarian crisis hampered media coverage, advocacy of women's rights, and investigations of violations of women's rights.

Female Genital Mutilation/Cutting (FGM/C): The law does not prohibit female genital mutilation/cutting (FGM/C), although a 2001 ministerial directive banned the practice in government institutions and medical facilities, according to HRW. The 2013 Demographic and Health Survey, administered by the Ministry of Public Health and Population, found that 19 percent of all women between the ages of 15 and 49 had undergone some form of FGM/C. A 2016 report of the UN Children's Fund (UNICEF) cited the same statistic. In some coastal areas influenced by cultural practices from the Horn of Africa, such as Mahara and Hudaydah, FGM/C practitioners had reportedly subjected up to 90 percent of women to FGM/C. UNICEF reported in 2012 that 97 percent of FGM/C procedures took place in the home and found Type 2, partial or total removal of the clitoris and the labia minora, with and without excision of the labia majora, in 83 percent of studied cases. The Women's National Committee and the Ministry of Endowments and Religious Guidance provided a manual for religious leaders on women's health problems, including the negative health consequences of FGM/C. A 2012 UNICEF report concluded that, despite an awareness campaign, the country still lagged in addressing the problem.

Other Harmful Traditional Practices: Cases of "honor" killing, the murder of a daughter or sister who "shamed" the family, occurred, particularly in rural areas. Most cases of honor killing went unreported, and authorities investigated very few instances. There were reports that family members murdered both male and female victims of rape or sexual abuse who reported the crime to protect the family's honor.

Sexual Harassment: No laws specifically prohibit sexual harassment, although the penal code criminalizes "shameful" or "immoral" acts. Authorities, however, rarely enforced the law. Sexual harassment in the streets was a major problem for women. A 2010 report by the Athar Foundation for Development, the most recent data available, found that 98.8 percent of women faced sexual harassment in the streets. The extent of sexual harassment was difficult to determine, and data was not available after the start of the conflict, although anecdotal reports, direct observation, and infrequent media reports suggested it also occurred in the workplace. There were anecdotal reports of employers transferring men accused of sexual harassment to other offices to prevent further abuse, although no further information was available.

Reproductive Rights: There were no reports of interference by the government in the right of couples and individuals to decide freely and responsibly the number, spacing, and timing of children, free from discrimination, coercion, and violence.

According to the UN Population Fund (UNFPA), 3.4 million women and girls of reproductive age were in need of humanitarian assistance, including 400,800 pregnant women. The conflict led to a breakdown of the health-care system, and women and girls did not have access to essential reproductive health services. UNFPA reported that access to maternal health care was also limited due to poverty, lack of health services, and low education on reproductive health and rights. According to UN estimates, the maternal mortality ratio was 385 deaths per 100,000 live births; there were 3,300 maternal deaths in 2015 and the lifetime risk of maternal death was one in 60. The majority of births took place at home, and only 45 percent of births were attended by skilled health personnel, according to 2016 UNFPA estimates. According to UNFPA, only 29 percent of women between the ages of 15 and 49 were using a modern method of contraceptives and 27 percent of women had an unmet need for family planning. Cultural taboos and misconceptions affected the contraceptive prevalence rate. Access to medications and pharmaceutical products also decreased due to the conflict. The adolescent birth rate remained high at 67 births per 1,000 women between the ages of 15 and 49, according to 2016 UNFPA estimates.

<u>Discrimination</u>: Women faced deeply entrenched discrimination in both law and practice in all aspects of their lives. Mechanisms to enforce equal protection were weak, and the government could not implement them effectively.

Women cannot marry without permission of their male guardians; do not have equal rights in inheritance, divorce, or child custody; and have little legal protection. Women do not enjoy the same legal status as men in family law, property law, inheritance law, and the judicial system. They experienced discrimination in areas such as employment, credit, pay, owning or managing businesses, education, and housing (see section 7.d.). The estimated 55 percent female literacy rate, compared with 85 percent for men, accentuated this discrimination. Prior to the conflict, women accounted for 30.5 percent of university students countrywide, and the NDC had adopted a 30 percent quota for admission of women to institutions of higher education; information was not available on whether this was implemented during the year.

A male relative's consent was often required before a woman could be admitted to a hospital, creating significant problems in a humanitarian context in which the men of the household were absent or had been killed.

Under family law and inheritance law, courts awarded custody of children over a specified age (seven years for boys and nine years for girls) to the divorced husband or the deceased husband's family. In numerous cases former husbands prevented divorced noncitizen women from visiting their children. Under sharia inheritance laws, which assume that women receive support from their male relatives, daughters receive half the inheritance and accidental death or injury compensation awarded to their brothers.

Women also faced unequal treatment in courts, where the testimony of a woman equals half that of a man's. Female parties in court proceedings, such as divorce and other family law cases, normally deputized male relatives to speak on their behalf, although they have the option to speak for themselves.

A husband may divorce a wife without justifying the action in court. In the formal legal system, a woman must provide justification. Under tribal customary law, however, a woman may divorce without justification.

Some local interpretations of sharia prohibit a Muslim woman from marrying a non-Muslim man, others permit marrying a Christian or Jewish man. All interpretations allow a Muslim man to marry a Christian or Jewish woman. The foreign wife of a male citizen must remain in the country for two years to obtain a residency permit.

Any citizen who wishes to marry a foreigner must obtain the permission of the Ministry of Interior (see section 1.f.). A woman wishing to marry a foreigner must present proof of her parents' approval. A foreign woman who wishes to marry a male citizen must prove to the ministry that she is "of good conduct and behavior."

Yemeni women may confer citizenship on children born of a foreign-born father if the child is born in the country. If the child is not born in the country, in rare cases the ministry may permit a woman to transmit citizenship to the child if the father dies or abandons the child (see section 6, Children).

Women experienced economic discrimination (see section 7.d.). Within the country's limited professional sphere, women had low rates of representation in a range of fields, including the security sector.

Children

Birth Registration: Citizenship derives from a child's parents. A child of a Yemeni father is a citizen. Yemeni women may confer citizenship on children born of a foreign-born father if the child is born in the country. If the child is not born in the country, in rare cases the Ministry of Interior may permit a woman to transmit citizenship to the child if the father dies or abandons the child.

There was no universal birth registration, and parents, especially in rural areas, never registered many children or registered them several years after birth. The requirement that children have birth certificates to register for school was not universally enforced, and there were no reports of authorities denying educational or health care services and benefits to children based on lack of registration.

Education: The law provides for universal, compulsory, and tuition-free education from ages six to 15. Public schooling was free to children through the secondary school level, but many children, especially girls, did not have easy access. According to a May *Humanitarian Situation Report* from UNICEF, around 30 percent (2.2 million) of school-age children in the country did not have access to education. The World Bank estimated more than three million children were out of school, in part due to the 1,600 schools that remained closed because of lack of security, physical damage, or their use as shelters for displaced persons.

Although attendance prior to the outbreak of the conflict was nominally mandatory through the ninth grade, only 79 percent of boys and 60 percent of girls attended primary school. The gender gap was larger for secondary and postsecondary schooling, with 34 percent of girls attending secondary school and only 6 percent continuing to postsecondary education. The lack of private toilet facilities for girls and reports of sexual harassment on the school commute contributed to the drop in girls' attendance after puberty.

School damage and destruction was particularly severe in the governorates of Hajjah, Marib, Sa'ada, Sana'a, and Ta'iz, where the conflict was particularly intense. According to a May *Humanitarian Situation Report* from UNICEF, nearly 530 schools remained closed in Ta'iz and Sa'ada. According to the UN Office for the Coordination of Humanitarians Affairs, as of June, some 1,600 schools remained closed due to conflict-related damages.

Medical Care: Due to social discrimination, male children received preferential medical treatment.

Child Abuse: The law does not define or prohibit child abuse, and there was no reliable data on its extent. Authorities considered violence against children a family affair, and tribal arbitration was more likely to handle it than reporting it to police.

Early and Forced Marriage: Early and forced marriage was a significant, widespread problem. The conflict likely exacerbated the situation, and representatives from local and international NGOs reported an increase in forced marriage and child marriage for financial reasons due to economic insecurity. There is no minimum age for marriage, and girls married as young as eight years of age, which traditionalists claimed served to assure they were virgins at the time of marriage. UNICEF's 2013 data estimated that 12 percent of females married by the age of 15 and 32 percent by the age of 18. The law forbids sex with underage brides until they are "suitable for sexual intercourse," an age that is undefined. An assessment undertaken by Intersos in Ta'iz in July 2015 found that 27 IDP and 10 host community families openly practiced early marriage, caused mostly by security concerns and local traditions.

Female Genital Mutilation/Cutting (FGM/C): Information is provided in the women's section above.

<u>Sexual Exploitation of Children</u>: The law does not define statutory rape and does not impose an age limit for consensual sex. The law prohibits pornography, including child pornography, although there was no information available on whether the legal prohibitions were comprehensive. Article 161 of the Child Rights Law criminalizes the prostitution of children.

Prior to the outbreak of conflict, observers reported the practice of foreigners visiting the country to enter into short-term marriages with young women and underage girls. In 2014 the Ministry of Interior attempted to stop the use of "temporary marriage" provisions of Islamic law as a vehicle for sex tourism (see section 1.f.). There were reports that elements within the government security forces exacted bribes and fees for facilitating temporary marriages. No information was available about related practices during the year.

<u>Child Soldiers</u>: See section 1.g., Child Soldiers.

<u>International Child Abductions</u>: The country is not a party to the 1980 Hague Convention on the Civil Aspects of International Child Abduction. See the Department of State's *Annual Report on International Parental Child Abduction* at travel.state.gov/content/childabduction/en/legal/compliance.html.

Anti-Semitism

Approximately 50 Jews remained in the country; according to media reports, most residing in a closed compound in Sana'a after the Israeli Jewish Agency succeeded in transporting 19 Jews to Israel in March. The continuing conflict further weakened law enforcement and put the Jewish community at risk, and many fled the country as a result. Prior to the outbreak of conflict, the transitional government continued to protect the Sa'ada Jewish community in Sana'a and provided secure housing and a living stipend.

See the Department of State's *International Religious Freedom Report* at www.state.gov/religiousfreedomreport/.

Anti-Semitic material was rare. Prior to the conflict, many Yemenis were proud to sustain a small Jewish community, with some charities reportedly donating food and gifts during Jewish holidays. Media coverage of the country's Jews was generally positive. The Houthi movement, however, adopted anti-Semitic slogans, including, "death to Israel, a curse on the Jews," and anti-Israeli rhetoric at times blurred into anti-Semitic utterances. Houthis continued to propagate such materials and slogans throughout the year, including adding anti-Israeli slogans and extremist rhetoric into elementary education curriculum and books.

Members of the Jewish community are not eligible to serve in the military or federal government. Authorities forbid them from carrying the ceremonial Yemeni dagger.

Trafficking in Persons

See the Department of State's *Trafficking in Persons Report* at www.state.gov/j/tip/rls/tiprpt/.

Persons with Disabilities

Several laws mandate the rights and care of persons with disabilities, but the government was unable to enforce them. The law permits persons with disabilities to exercise the same rights as persons without disabilities, but this did not happen in practice. Prior to the outbreak of conflict, social stigma and official indifference were obstacles to implementation.

The law reserves 5 percent of government jobs for persons with disabilities and mandates the acceptance of persons with disabilities in universities, exempts them from paying tuition, and requires that schools be made more accessible to persons with disabilities. The extent to which any authority implemented these laws was unclear.

Children with disabilities may attend public schools, although schools make no special accommodations for them. There were some private educational institutions for persons with disabilities in large cities. Many parents refused to send their children with disabilities to public schools, due to concern about potential harassment. The conflict likely further reduced access to schools.

Although the law mandates that new buildings have access for persons with disabilities, compliance was poor. Most persons with disabilities relied on their extended family for support.

Information about patterns of abuse of persons with disabilities in educational and mental health institutions was not publicly available.

Prior to the outbreak of conflict, authorities imprisoned persons with mental disabilities with criminals without providing adequate medical care and in some instances without legal charge. At that time, the Ministry of Interior reported that family members sometimes brought relatives with mental disabilities to ministry-run prisons and asked officers to imprison them. Ministry-run prisons in Sana'a, Aden, and Ta'iz operated semiautonomous units for prisoners with mental disabilities in cooperation with the Red Crescent Society. Conditions in these units reportedly were deficient in cleanliness and professional care.

The Ministry of Social Affairs and Labor is responsible for protecting the rights of persons with disabilities. The government-in-exile could not continue collaboration with the World Bank to administer a social development fund; the ministry was also unable to oversee the Fund for the Care and Rehabilitation of the Disabled, which provided limited basic services and supported more than 60 NGOs assisting persons with disabilities.

National/Racial/Ethnic Minorities

Although racial discrimination is illegal, some groups, such as the Muhamasheen or Akhdam community, and the Muwaladeen (Yemenis born to foreign parents), faced social and institutional discrimination based on race, ethnicity, and social status. The Muhamasheen, who traditionally provided low-prestige services such as street sweeping, generally lived in poverty and endured persistent societal discrimination. Muhamasheen women were particularly vulnerable to rape and other abuse because of the general impunity for attackers due to the women's low-caste status. In 2013 the NDC's Rights and Freedoms Working group announced agreement on measures to protect the rights of the Muhamasheen and to ban discrimination against them, but it was not known whether any of these measures were implemented.

Acts of Violence, Discrimination, and Other Abuses Based on Sexual Orientation and Gender Identity

Lesbian, gay, bisexual, transgender, and intersex (LGBTI) persons faced discrimination and could face the death penalty, although there were no known executions of LGBTI persons in more than a decade. The penal code criminalizes consensual same-sex sexual conduct, with the death penalty as a sanction under the country's interpretation of Islamic law.

Due to the illegality of and possible severe punishment for consensual same-sex sexual conduct, there were no LGBTI organizations. Because the law does not prohibit discrimination, the government did not consider LGBTI problems "relevant" for official reporting, and few LGBTI persons were open about their sexual orientation or gender identity. The government blocked access to LGBTI internet sites.

HIV and AIDS Social Stigma

While there were no reports of social violence against persons with HIV/AIDS, the topic was socially sensitive and infrequently discussed. Discrimination against persons with HIV/AIDS is a criminal offense, and information was not available on whether there were reports of incidents of discrimination occurring during the year.

Section 7. Worker Rights

Government enforcement of labor law was weak to nonexistent due to the continuing conflict. Labor laws were still in effect, but Houthi-Saleh rebels controlled the ministries responsible for their implementation, and the government was unable to enforce them. Little information on labor conditions during the year was available.

a. Freedom of Association and the Right to Collective Bargaining

The labor code provides for the right of salaried private sector employees to organize and bargain collectively without government interference. These protections do not apply to public servants, day laborers, domestic servants, foreign workers, and other groups who together made up the majority of the work force. The civil service code covers public servants. The law generally protects employees from antiunion discrimination and prohibits dismissal for union activities. Due to the conflict, the government lacked the capacity to enforce labor laws effectively.

While unions may negotiate wage settlements for their members and may conduct strikes or other actions to achieve their demands, workers have the right to strike only if prior attempts at negotiation and arbitration fail. They must give advance notice to the employer and government and receive prior written approval from the executive office of the General Federation of Unions of the Republic. Strikes may not be carried out for "political purposes."

The Ministry of Social Affairs and Labor has veto power over collective bargaining agreements. Employees may appeal any dispute, including cases of antiunion discrimination, to the ministry. Employees also may take a case to the Labor Arbitration Committee, which the ministry chairs, composed of an employer representative and a representative of the General Federation of the Yemeni Workers' Trade Unions (GFYWTU). Parties generally preferred to resolve cases via the committee system, since court proceedings were costly and the judicial system was often corrupt.

According to the GFYWTU, the government allowed public sector employees, especially those employed in ministries, to unionize and strike if the unions had more than 200 members. Otherwise, authorities prohibited public employees from unionizing, and they had to take labor grievances to court.

Although not required by law, all unions were federated within the GFYWTU. While not formally affiliated with the government, the GFYWTU was the only official federation and worked with the government to resolve labor disputes.

The law requires a minimum of 18 employees to establish a union in a workplace. The majority of private-sector employers registered only five to 10 employees, allowing them to avoid many social security and labor union regulations. Companies with more than 100 employees comprised fewer than 100,000 persons. Union sources stated the private sector had begun to recognize the benefit of working with unions to meet employee demands. Prior to the outbreak of conflict, penalties were generally sufficient to deter violations.

The government was unable to enforce laws on freedom of association and the right to collective bargaining.

Prior to the outbreak of the conflict, the government at times sought to influence unions by inserting its own personnel into them. In some instances, political parties also attempted to control unions and professional associations by influencing internal elections or placing their own personnel in them, usually tied to the government.

In practical terms, a union's ability to strike depended on its political strength. Under the transitional government, authorities often accused unions and associations of being linked to a political party. The Development Working Group of the NDC called for the independence of all unions.

b. Prohibition of Forced or Compulsory Labor

The penal code prescribes up to 10 years' imprisonment for any person who "buys, sells, gives [a human being] as a present, or deals in human beings; and anyone who brings into the country or exports from it a human being with the intent of taking advantage of him." This statue's narrow focus on transactions and movement means the law does not criminalize many forms of forced labor.

Prior to the outbreak of conflict, the government did not effectively enforce the law due to lack of resources and financial interests of the elite, many of whom supported such forms of labor. Once in exile, authorities could not enforce the law.

There were numerous reports of such practices in both urban and rural areas. Some sources reported that the practice of chattel slavery in which human beings were traded as property continued. While no official statistics existed detailing this practice, a 2014 study by a human rights organization documented 190 cases of slavery in three directorates of Hajjah Governorate. Sources report there could be several hundred other men, women, and children sold or inherited as slaves in al-Hodeida and al-Mahwit Governorates. In some instances employers forced children into domestic servitude and agricultural work (see section 7.c.) and women into domestic servitude or prostitution. Migrant workers were vulnerable to forced labor conditions.

See also the Department of State's *Trafficking in Persons Report* at www.state.gov/j/tip/rls/tiprpt/.

c. Prohibition of Child Labor and Minimum Age for Employment

The law prohibits child labor, but the government was unable to implement its regulations effectively. Poverty, disruption of services due to conflict, and lack of resources posed a serious challenge to the law. The Combating Child Labor Unit (CCLU) within the Ministry of Social Affairs and Labor was responsible for implementing and enforcing child labor laws and regulations.

The International Labor Organization (ILO) characterized the country's minimum work age as "the minimum age for admission to employment which is free of any hazards may not be lower than the age of completion of compulsory education and may not be less than 14 years."

Children under 18 with formal contracts may work no longer than six hours a day, with a one-hour break after four consecutive hours, on weekdays between 7 a.m. and 7 p.m.

Child labor was common, including its worst forms. According to a 2013 ILO study, more than 1.3 million children participated in the workforce, including 469,000 children between the ages of five and 11. The results of the country's 2012 national child labor survey indicated that 17 percent of the 7.7 million children in the five to 17 age group and 11 percent of those between the ages of five and 11 were involved in child labor. In 2014 the director of the CCLU estimated the informal minimum wages paid by private sector businesses to children ranged between 430 and 650 riyals ($1.70 to $2.60) per day.

UNICEF reported in May that approximately 30 percent of school-age children in the country do not have access to education (see section 6, Children). Many children of school age worked instead of attending school, particularly in areas where schools were not easily accessible or closed due to conflict. In rural areas, family poverty and traditional practice led many children to work in subsistence farming. In urban areas, children worked in stores and workshops, sold goods, and begged on the streets. Children also worked in some industries and construction. According to the Ministry of Social Affairs and Labor, small factories and shops sometimes employed children outside the family, particularly in rural areas. Continued weak economic conditions forced hundreds of children to seek work in the hazardous fishery sector. Children also reportedly worked in dangerous conditions in construction, offshore fishing, mining, and waste dumps. According to HRW, nearly one-third of all combatants in the country were under 18 years of age (see section 1.g., Child Soldiers).

Penalties existed to punish the worst forms of child labor, and the government made minimal enforcement efforts. No information was available on arrests, investigations, or prosecutions for child labor offenses. If inspectors found child labor violations, authorities resolved most cases between inspectors and employers with a verbal warning and by working with the employer to change the child's job to remove the child from danger.

See also the Department of Labor's *Findings on the Worst Forms of Child Labor* at www.dol.gov/ilab/reports/child-labor/findings/.

d. Discrimination with Respect to Employment and Occupation

Labor laws and regulations prohibit discrimination with regard to race, sex, color, beliefs, language, or disability and specifically provide that "women shall be equal with men in relation to conditions of employment and employment rights." The law does not address sexual orientation, political opinion, national origin, social origin, gender identity, HIV status, or other communicable diseases. Authorities did not consistently enforce the laws, and discrimination based on race, gender, and disability remained a serious problem in employment and occupation.

Prior to the conflict, women's rights activists and NGOs reported discrimination was a common practice in the public and private sectors. Women experienced discrimination in areas such as employment, credit, pay, owning or managing businesses, education, and housing. Prior to the conflict, women and girls who were 15 or older represented only 25 percent of the formal workforce, largely due to barriers to education and social traditions that precluded women from seeking and gaining employment. Cultural barriers also restricted the exercise of women's property rights. In most rural areas, social norms largely prevented women from owning land.

Racial and employment discrimination against the Muhamasheen was a problem. Persons with disabilities faced discrimination in hiring and access to workplace.

e. Acceptable Conditions of Work

There was no established minimum wage in the private sector. The minimum civil service wage was 21,000 riyals ($84) per month; government agencies implemented it. The labor law provides equal wages for public sector workers employed in joint ventures between the government and the private sector.

The law specifies a maximum 48-hour workweek with a maximum eight-hour workday, although many workshops and stores operated 10- to 12-hour shifts without penalty. The 35-hour workweek for government employees was nominally seven hours per day from Sunday through Thursday. The law requires overtime pay, paid holidays and leave, and prohibits excessive or compulsory overtime.

The law prescribes occupational, safety, and health standards. It states every employer must provide safe and healthy conditions for workers. The law recognizes the right of workers to remove themselves from dangerous work situations, and workers may challenge dismissals based on such actions in court.

There were no reported instances of this during the year. The law provides for compensation in the event of work accidents or death. The safety law does not apply to domestic servants, casual workers, or agricultural workers.

The Ministry of Social Affairs and Labor's vocational safety department relied on inspection committees to conduct primary and periodic safety and health investigations. A lack of funding and resources, such as vehicles to travel to inspection sites, as well as conflict constrained such committees. Some foreign-owned companies and major manufacturers implemented higher health, safety, and environmental standards than the government requires. The Ministry of Oil has monitoring responsibility for oil-related businesses. There was no credible information available regarding work-related accidents or fatalities during the year. Government enforcement of labor law was weak to nonexistent. Working conditions generally were poor, and wage and overtime violations were common. Foreign migrant workers, youth, and female workers typically faced the most exploitative working conditions.